D0466351

Little Pebble™

What Are Hurricanes?

by Mari Schuh

PEBBLE
a capstone imprint

Little Pebble is published by Pebble
1710 Roe Crest Drive,
North Mankato, Minnesota 56003
www.mycapstone.com

Library of Congress Cataloging-in-Publication Data
Names: Schuh, Mari C., 1975–author.
Title: What are hurricanes? / by Mari Schuh.
Description: North Mankato, Minnesota : Pebble, a
 Capstone imprint, [2019] | Series: Little pebble.
 Wicked weather | Audience: Ages 4–8.
Identifiers: LCCN 2018029836 (print) | LCCN
 2018031695 (ebook) | ISBN 9781977103345
 (eBook PDF) | ISBN 9781977103277 (hardcover) |
 ISBN 9781977105448 (paperback)
Subjects: LCSH: Hurricanes—Juvenile literature.
Classification: LCC QC944.2 (ebook) | LCC QC944.2
 .S393 2019 (print) | DDC 551.55/2—dc23
LC record available at https://lccn.loc.gov/2018029836

Editorial Credits
Nikki Potts, editor, Kyle Grenz, designer;
Heather Mauldin, media researcher; Tori Abraham, production specialist

Photo Credits
Alamy: Dennis MacDonald, 11; Getty Images: Ian Cumming, 13,
Paul Chesley, 21, Warren Faidley, 15; iStockphoto: Maryna Patzen, 7;
Shutterstock: Brandon Bourdages, cover, Drew McArthur, 1, Mia2you, 19,
Multiverse, 17, Trong Nguyen, 9, Valentin Ayupov, 5

Printed and bound in China.
000966

Table of Contents

What Is a Hurricane?

Look at the ocean.

Storm clouds spin in the sky.

It is a hurricane!

A hurricane is a tropical storm.

It forms over warm oceans.

It has a center.

It is called the eye.

The eye is a calm spot.

eye

Every hurricane has a name.
Why?
Then it is easy to track
each one.

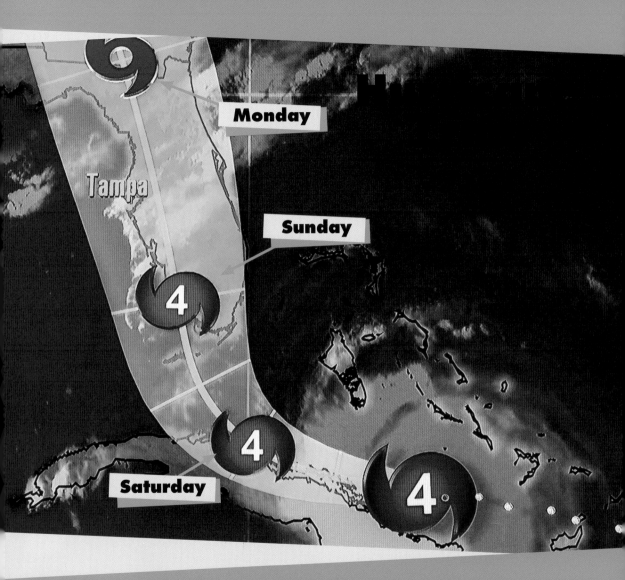

tracking map of Hurricane Irma

Look out!

Hurricanes can move

over land.

They bring wind and rain.

13

Huge waves hit the shore.

Water floods homes and cities.

Be safe!

Strong winds blow.
They pull trees out of
the ground.

Staying Safe

People get ready.

They cover windows

with boards.

Boards help keep homes safe.

Experts watch for storms.

They tell people to get

to safety.

Go now!

NATIONAL HURRICANE CENTER

Glossary

calm—quiet and peaceful

expert—a person with great skill or who knows a lot about something

eye—the calm area at the center of a hurricane

hurricane—a strong, swirling wind and rainstorm that starts on the ocean

shore—the place where the ocean meets land

storm—bad weather; hurricanes, tornadoes, and blizzards are types of storms

tropical—having to do with the hot and wet areas near the equator

Read More

Baker, John R. *The World's Worst Hurricanes.* Mankato, Minn. Capstone Press, 2017.

Gregory, Josh. *If You Were a Kid Surviving a Hurricane.* New York: Children's Press, 2018.

Rivera, Andrea. *Hurricanes.* Zoom in on Natural Disasters. Minneapolis: Abdo Zoom, 2018.

Internet Sites

Use FactHound to find Internet sites related to this book.

Visit www.facthound.com

Just type in 9781977103277 and go.

Super-cool stuff!

Check out projects, games and lots more at **www.capstonekids.com**

Critical Thinking Questions

1. Where do hurricanes form?

2. How can people stay safe during a hurricane?

3. What is the middle of a hurricane called?

Index